WOULD YOU RATHER
Gift Game Book

For Kids
6-12 Years
Old

WOULD YOU RATHER

Dye eggs on Halloween
or trick-or-treat
on Easter?

Arrange an Easter egg hunt
or create a fort
out of cardboard boxes?

WOULD YOU RATHER

Collect eggshells
or sugar packets?

Cook macaroni and cheese
or cheesy potatoes?

WOULD YOU RATHER

Spend a month
without candies
or without cartoons?

Choose one gift
or get ten
random presents?

WOULD YOU RATHER

Be a famous musician
or a firefighter?

Find a buried
treasure chest
or discover an island
with unknown animals?

WOULD YOU RATHER

Be a ballerina
or a detective?

Turn into a whale
or an elephant?

WOULD YOU RATHER

Eat sliced pears
or baby carrots?

Have your father's
or your mother's birthday
on Easter?

WOULD YOU RATHER

Turn into a unicorn or a dragon on weekends?

Eat avocado rolls or watermelon pizza?

WOULD YOU RATHER

Have a parrot or a lizard as a pet?

Be a horse or a pony?

WOULD YOU RATHER

Sneeze every minute or walk with your eyes closed in your room?

Have the sheep fur or llama fur on your head?

WOULD YOU RATHER

Have a giraffe's neck or have no neck at all?

Be smaller than a mouse or larger than a T-Rex?

WOULD YOU RATHER

Clean the castle
with 100 bedrooms or
the entire football stadium?

Always wear super dark
sunglasses at night or
a headlight helmet
during the day?

WOULD YOU RATHER

Have a full-sized basketball court or a merry-go-round carousel in your backyard?

Read a scary book or a very boring book?

WOULD YOU RATHER

Get a giant cotton candy or
blow the world's
largest gum bubble?

Grow a Christmas tree or
an Easter basket
on your head?

WOULD YOU
RATHER

Eat watermelon with salt or
a banana with pepper?

Eat raw egg or
skittles with chopsticks?

WOULD YOU RATHER

Be able to see well
in the dark
or climb up trees
like a cat?

Invent the Internet
or the first spaceship?

WOULD YOU RATHER

Play with a dolphin or
with a baby elephant?

Spend an hour in a bear's or
a lion's den?

WOULD YOU
RATHER

Eat zucchini ice cream or eggplant pie?

Drink a spoon of onion or garlic juice?

WOULD YOU RATHER

Everyday do pull-ups on an exercise bar or do cartwheels?

Live a month in the body of a monkey or a toucan?

WOULD YOU RATHER

Travel to London or Paris?

Have thirty rainy or snowy days in a row next week?

WOULD YOU RATHER

Fall into a swimming pool or into a lake?

Live in the Hobbit House or the upside down house?

WOULD YOU RATHER

Pet a kangaroo or
an aardvark?

See an albino tiger or
an albino giraffe?

WOULD YOU RATHER

Hide a kitten or
a puppy from your teacher
in a class?

Own a hot dog-shaped
jet ski or
a duckling-shaped boat?

WOULD YOU RATHER

Make twenty pancakes or
twenty beds
every morning?

Mow a lawn or
vacuum five bedrooms
every day?

WOULD YOU RATHER

**Read or write
one page per second?**

**Ride a horse or
an elephant to school?**

WOULD YOU RATHER

Have a zipline
from your home to school
or shopping mall?

Play barefoot hockey or
ride a bike barefoot?

WOULD YOU RATHER

Watch a sunrise
or a sunset
on the Moon?

Speak Italian or French?

WOULD YOU RATHER

Invent a new language or build a new computer program?

Live in the world without washing machines or without fridges?

WOULD YOU RATHER

Sleep in a McDonald's or at a bus stop?

Sleep in your warmest clothes or go for a walk in your pajamas when it's snowing?

WOULD YOU RATHER

Have an elephant's tail or trunk on your body?

Fly on a huge drone or explore the ocean in a submarine?

WOULD YOU RATHER

Be able to hold your breath
for one hour
or live without food
and water for one year?

Win an Olympic medal or
get in the
Guinness Book
of World Records?

WOULD YOU RATHER

Own a pink cat
or a green dog?

Control the rain
or the wind?

WOULD YOU RATHER

Play yard twister or
water balloon piñata?

Become a professional
painter or dancer?

WOULD YOU RATHER

Be a master in crocheting or knitting?

Plant a unique flower or discover a new planet?

WOULD YOU RATHER

Be unable to fall asleep
or feel sleepy all the time?

Grow strawberries
which taste like bananas
or bananas which taste
like strawberries?

WOULD YOU RATHER

Be a football or
a basketball superstar?

Turn invisible
when you are angry
or when you are surprised?

WOULD YOU RATHER

Be invincible to snakes
or sharks?

Only be able to eat
with plastic forks
or paper spoons?

WOULD YOU RATHER

Sleep or sneeze with your eyes open?

Eat plenty of garlic or onions before having a birthday party?

WOULD YOU RATHER

Enjoy your birthday cake with ketchup or mustard?

Be raised by wolves or bears?

WOULD YOU RATHER

Have seven sisters
and one brother
or vice versa?

Bark like a dog
or meow like a cat
when you are surprised?

WOULD YOU RATHER

Brush your teeth
or wash your body
upside down?

Meet a T-Rex
or a Bigfoot
near your house?

WOULD YOU RATHER

Become an English teacher
in a small village
in your country or a big city
in another country?

Be a professional
photographer
or a fashion designer?

WOULD YOU RATHER

Live in a transparent house
or a house
with chicken legs?

Make friends
with a talking cookie
or with a talking sponge?

WOULD YOU
RATHER

Wear gloves on your feet
or socks on your arms
when it's cold?

Wear a shirt
with a design of red alligators
or orange iguanas?

WOULD YOU RATHER

Run half an hour
when it's raining
or when it's snowing?

Get a free ticket
to the movie theater
or football match?

WOULD YOU RATHER

Go to the dentist
or clean your house
every day?

Become a baby sitter
or a dog walker?

WOULD YOU RATHER

Learn the name
of every plant
or every animal?

Burn hundreds of letters
in a fireplace
or cut them
into small pieces?

WOULD YOU
RATHER

Take care of lilies
or orchids in the garden?

Become your mom
or your grandma for a day?

WOULD YOU RATHER

Become your dad
or your grandpa for a day?

Time travel into the future
or to the past?

WOULD YOU RATHER

**Build a UFO
or a rocket from a kit?**

**Spend a year
in a very remote
mountain village
or on an
uninhabited island?**

WOULD YOU RATHER

Survive on apples
or bananas for a week?

Dance near the pyramids
in Egypt or Mexico?

WOULD YOU RATHER

Wake up in a wet bed or because of hearing gunshots?

Play soap boat races or an obstacle course in the yard?

WOULD YOU RATHER

Wear a Lady Bug
or Pikachu costume
every time you go out?

Wear Ninja Turtles
or Paw Patrol costumes
when at school
with your classmates?

WOULD YOU
RATHER

Swap bodies
with your best friend
or with a random student
at your school for a day?

Learn how to play the guitar
or the piano?

WOULD YOU RATHER

Build paper houses or paper animals like a pro?

Help to build a house or grow a garden?

WOULD YOU RATHER

Brush your teeth
or wash your hair
once a month?

Make three snowmen
or one hundred snowballs?

WOULD YOU RATHER

Sleep on the floor
or in a garage?

Design calendars
or book covers?

WOULD YOU RATHER

Live without towels
or a toothbrush?

Never wear socks
or sunglasses?

WOULD YOU RATHER

Always drink from your hands or eat with your hands?

Be a helicopter or an airplane pilot?

WOULD YOU RATHER

Be the strongest
or the smartest person
on the planet?

Go to school
even on weekends
or never be able
to eat meat?

WOULD YOU RATHER

Always wear grey or yellow clothes?

Wear a sleep mask or ear muffs from 1 to 2 pm every day?

WOULD YOU RATHER

Spend your birthday morning
climbing a mountain
or walking in the forest?

Meet your favorite
actress or actor?

WOULD YOU RATHER

Sometimes have very realistic nightmares or never have dreams at all?

Never feel tired or never feel hungry?

WOULD YOU RATHER

Perform on stage
in a cruise liner
or in an opera house?

Spend an hour
at a bus stop
or three hours
in a traffic jam?

WOULD YOU
RATHER

Take part in a swimming race
or a horse race?

Hold a chameleon
or a gecko
on your shoulder?

WOULD YOU RATHER

Watch weather forecasts or football predictions on TV?

Have to remember phone numbers or birthdays for each of your acquaintances?

WOULD YOU RATHER

Be very shy
or easily distracted?

Be a big wild animal
or a small domestic animal?

WOULD YOU RATHER

Always have a clean nose or clean ears?

Eat your meal with lots of salt or pepper?

WOULD YOU RATHER

Wake up with the sun or go to sleep at sunset?

Go fishing or hunting on your day-off?

WOULD YOU RATHER

Roast marshmallows in a SpongeBob or Winnie-the-Pooh costume?

Care for abandoned cats or donate your old toys to a charity?

WOULD YOU RATHER

See fireworks every day
or have a Ferris Wheel
near your house?

Model a life-size
play-doh pizza
or ice cream sundae?

WOULD YOU RATHER

Hear a new joke
every time
you scratch your nose
or your ear?

Dance with a baby bear
or with a baby monkey?

WOULD YOU RATHER

Sleep in a room
with a huge spider
or a snake?

Live in a tent at Disney World
or at a luxury villa in Alaska?

WOULD YOU RATHER

Clap your hands uncontrollably whenever someone falls or sneezes?

Sing a song for your parents every night or every morning?

WOULD YOU RATHER

Make up imaginary stories about aliens or unicorns?

Be a part-time policeman or a firefighter?

WOULD YOU RATHER

**Film a 3D movie
or be filmed in a 3D movie?**

**Have a cool hammock
or a giant box of Legos?**

WOULD YOU RATHER

Be the country's best skater
or a snowboarder?

Spend a day
in a huge aquarium
or in the jungle?

WOULD YOU RATHER

Model tiny airplanes or helicopters?

Take photos of a UFO or an alien?

WOULD YOU RATHER

Build a snowman in summer or surf in winter?

Get transparent shoes or a transparent school bag?

WOULD YOU RATHER

Have a twin brother
or twin sister?

Make a wooden tray
or a photo frame?

WOULD YOU RATHER

Experience an earthquake or a hurricane?

Have a flying umbrella or a flying carpet?

WOULD YOU RATHER

Play the violin
or the drums?

Draw mazes
or invent funny words?

WOULD YOU RATHER

Visit the world's
best 100 beaches
or best 100 restaurants?

Live in a world
full of giant butterflies
or miniature giraffes?

WOULD YOU RATHER

Have a spaceship-shaped
or a shark-shaped
bean bag chair?

Be the oldest kid
in your class
or win at every
board game you play?

WOULD YOU RATHER

Own a hot air balloon
or a haunted house?

Get a huge box
of fortune cookies
or a cotton candy machine?

WOULD YOU RATHER

Have a bouncy castle
or a porch swing?

Take a bath in a waterfall
or swim in the infinity pool?

WOULD YOU RATHER

Win a ton of bubble gum
or a ton of crackers?

Get a new jet ski
or an iPhone
covered with gold?

WOULD YOU RATHER

Pop bubble wrap
or solve funny crosswords?

Play shadow puppets
or make mud pies?

WOULD YOU RATHER

Spend a night in a treehouse
or a lighthouse?

Watch a meteor shower
or see planets
through a telescope?

WOULD YOU
RATHER

Be unable to see
or be unable to hear
for a minute?

Have a pillow fight
or build sandcastles
with your friends?

WOULD YOU RATHER

Have a sunrise breakfast
at the beach
or in the forest?

Make a hand-painted
Hawaiian shirt or a hoodie?

WOULD YOU RATHER

Make homemade mini donuts
or mini pizzas?

Paint your room
or your parents' room?

WOULD YOU RATHER

Play classic bowling
or bottle bowling
in a rooftop café?

Run a three-legged race
or egg-and-spoon race?

WOULD YOU RATHER

Have a ten-hour walk
in a beautiful old town
or a beautiful spring forest?

Be a famous
YouTube blogger
or an Instagram blogger?

WOULD YOU RATHER

Teach your friends how to finger paint or to decorate jeans?

Do fun science experiments or learn some magic tricks?

WOULD YOU RATHER

Be in a small boat
on the ocean
or a hot air balloon
during a storm?

Make yourself a spider
or shark face painting?

WOULD YOU RATHER

Take photos of insects or flowers?

Make up trivia questions or collect random facts?

WOULD YOU RATHER

Take a hot honey bath
or a hot chocolate bath?

Listen to scary stories
about ghosts
or monsters?

WOULD YOU RATHER

Walk a mile barefoot
or walk in your pajamas
and sneakers
on a snowy day?

Imitate animal sounds
or vehicle sounds?

WOULD YOU RATHER

Eat a mango
or a grapefruit every hour?

Cook breakfasts
or dinners every day?

WOULD YOU RATHER

Always sleep
on seven pillows
or sleep on the floor?

Learn about dinosaurs
or the first humans
from a science
encyclopedia?

WOULD YOU RATHER

Have a popular YouTube channel about growing carrots or cabbages on Mars?

Sleep on a bookshelf or do your homework in the bathroom?

THE END

PLEASE,
LEAVE YOUR
REVIEWS!

Made in the USA
Middletown, DE
28 March 2020